FAITHFUL

- In All His Ways

Steve Martin

Copyright © 2016 by Steve Martin

Book Title: Faithful – In All His Ways

This is the 13th book by Steve Martin.

ISBN-13: **978-1537755656**
ISBN-10: **153775565X**

Printed in the United States of America

All rights reserved solely by the author. The author guarantees all contents are original and do not infringe upon the legal rights of any other person or work. No part of this book may be reproduced in any form without the permission of the author.

The views expressed in this book are those of the author and publisher, Martin Lighthouse Publishing.

Book cover by Steve Martin
Photos by Steve Martin (except for the one he is in!)

www.loveforhispeople@blogspot.com

Bible quotations are taken from the following versions:

The New King James Version. Copyright © 1982 by Thomas Nelson, Inc. Used by permission. All rights reserved.

The New American Standard Version, Copyright © 1960, 1962, 1963, 1968, 1971, 1972, 1973, 1975, 1977, 1995 by the Lockman Foundation. Used by permission. All rights reserved.

The Complete Jewish Bible, and English Version of the Tanakh (Old Testament) and B'rit Hadashah (New Testament) by Jewish New Testament Publications, Inc., Clarksville, Maryland USA.

The Message. Copyright ©1993, 1994, 1995, 1996, 2000, 2001, 2002. Used by permission of NavPress Publishing Group. Used by permission. All rights reserved.

TABLE OF CONTENTS

Dedication   Page 6
Introduction   Page 7

1. Cloak of Deception
   -The Dream and Reality   Page 9
2. Let the Dead Bury the Dead   Page 13
3. A Lighthouse & Watchman   Page 19
4. Little Things   Page 22
5. When It Hasn't Happened Yet   Page 25
6. Soft & Tender   Page 29
7. I Want It   Page 33
8. Tilt Your Head Up   Page 37
9. Held By Your Love Lord   Page 40
10. Silence Is Golden   Page 44
11. What If   Page 48
12. Take The Time   Page 53
13. Steps Along The Way   Page 55
14. Faithful   Page 57
15. Israel & Our Friends   Page 60
16. Being Faithful   Page 63
17. Cycles   Page 65
18. Dogs   Page 69
19. Inquire of the Lord   Page 72
20. Work Is Work   Page 75
21. The Elections   Page 78
22. Let Not Your Heart Grow Cold   Page 81
23. What To Do   Page 84
24. History & Truth   Page 87

ABOUT THE AUTHOR   Page 89

CONTACT INFORMATION   Page 91

**OTHER BOOKS
  BY STEVE MARTIN**   Page 93

*Stop the Boycott of Israeli Goodies
 - Buy Israeli Hoodies!*   Page 108

DEDICATION

I dedicate this book to those who have gone before us, leading the way, and to those who stand with us in these days, who will be faithful to the end.

INTRODUCTION

Continuing with another book edition of my latest inspirational writings of **Now Think of This**, I hope you are encouraged in your daily faith, to be faithful, as our Lord Jesus is faithful in all His ways.

Our main example and inspiration is the Lord Jesus Himself, Who was faithful to the end. Others that have followed since His time on earth have stood for the truth He spoke. We do well to keep our eyes stayed on Him, so we too can practice faithfulness in the days, which I believe are near the end as the Bible speaks of before His promised return.

My prayer is that these short messages will help build your faith, stand for truth, and continue to be a light in the darkness that seeks to cover the earth.

The Lord Jesus is coming back, as the Lion of Judah, the King of kings and the Lord of lords. All eyes will see Him in the clouds, riding His mighty stead, the One Who is Faithful and True.

Even so, come Lord Yeshua.

Shalom,

Steve Martin
Charlotte, NC

1.

Cloak of Deception
-The Dream and Reality

"…the one whose coming is in accord with the activity of Satan, with all power and signs and false wonders, and with all the deception of wickedness for those who perish, because they did not receive the love of the truth so as to be saved." (2 Thessalonians 2:9-11 NASU)

The dream kept repeating itself, even as I was waking up. Over and over again, the same thing was going through my head. It was a commercial being shown on TV. During the Super Bowl none the less, when millions were watching, unaware of what was really happening. Their homes were wide open to this cloak of deception.

What I remembered most from the dream was its ending. Pictured on the TV screen were two young boys, having a good time playing, unaware of this evil cloud coming over them. It was a gay, immoral spirit. They kept on playing, completely innocent of what was happening about them.

And then the most troubling aspect of this dream was that this demonic spirit came right through the TV, into the living rooms of the millions watching the commercial. Having found an "open door", the evil spirit from hell was free to bring its presence into the family house. Those viewing that moment, thinking it was just another "super commercial", were passively, totally unaware of what had just happened. Then I woke up.

This is one of the spiritual movements overtaking our nation. It is an evil one. And even as the story goes of the frog slowly being boiled alive, as the temperature rises in the cooking pot eventually to the point where he no longer is aware of his impending death, so the countries of the world are succumbing to deception. And then they will accept anything, and anyone, who comes along in disguise.

What is going on in America and elsewhere is just this. Sitting by and watching the level of innocence drop over the last decades, what used to be known as clearly being black and white sin is now accepted as the norm, the "way love should be expressed", the "let it be let it be" accepted reality. We have been given over to a spirit of delusion – the very cloak of deception.

"Do you not remember that when I was still with you I told you these things? And now you know what is restraining, that he may be revealed in his own time. For the mystery of lawlessness is already at work; only He who now restrains will do so until He is taken out of the way. And then the lawless one will be revealed, whom the Lord will consume with the breath of His mouth and destroy with the brightness of His coming.

The coming of the lawless one is according to the working of Satan, with all power, signs, and lying wonders, and with all unrighteous deception among those who perish, because they did not receive the love of the truth, that they might be saved. And for this reason God will send them strong delusion, that they should believe the lie, that they all may be condemned who did not believe the truth but had pleasure in unrighteousness." (2 Thessalonians 2:5-12 NKJV)

How many in the nations have opened themselves up to the spirits of deception, those lying spirits of the evil one, by slowly receiving into their souls, their spirits, their homes, the very lies that can destroy their spiritual lives? As the years have passed, they have succumbed to the enveloping evil cloud, by what they have allowed themselves to be exposed to, and given acceptance of. Evil has found its way through the cracked doors, displayed quietly in ever increasing and accepting measures on the movie screen and the TV shows, as the perversion in sex, drugs and gay lifestyle have been approved within the "enlightened" times we live in.

How are you stopping your kids, your grandkids, from being overtaken with the slow destruction of the enemy? Are you allowing yourself, and them, to sit idly by and let this cloak of deception cover your house and come into your home? Overtaking your life and theirs?

What will you do, and when, will you stop it?

If your life is not founded on biblical truths, on the solid rock that never changes, then you too are exposing yourself to this very thing. And when the time comes to stand against the onslaught of the enemy, you too will give in to its grip. It may be too late.

Prepare yourself now, and those you love, by knowing the Truth and standing strong on His Word. His name is Jesus. Only in Him will you be able to stand.

2.

Let the Dead Bury the Dead

"Yeshua said, "Let the dead bury their own dead; you, go and proclaim the Kingdom of God!" (Luke 9:60-61 Complete Jewish Bible)

For years I had thought this was a rather harsh response Jesus (Yeshua) gave to the one who said he wanted to follow Him and be His disciple. Jesus didn't say, "Great! Just come along, do what you want when you want, and I will be sure to accommodate how you live so it won't cramp your style." It even seems in some circles that our response nowadays would be, "Wow! Someone who wants to be a Christian! Let's not make it too hard on them so they won't start the walk and then later quit. We need all the ones we can get."

No, Jesus gave the man the one choice he had. Follow Him by letting go of his current life, and live the one I (Jesus) would direct him in. My way is the only way.

Jesus clearly told the one the way it would be, as Luke recounted for us in this historical report.

"As they were going along the road, someone said to Him, "I will follow You wherever You go." And Jesus said to him, "The foxes have holes and the birds of the air have nests, but the Son of Man has nowhere to lay His head." And He said to another, " Follow Me." But he said, "Lord, permit me first to go and bury my father." But He said to him, "Allow the dead to bury their own dead; but as for you, go and proclaim everywhere the kingdom of God."

Another also said, "I will follow You, Lord; but first permit me to say good-bye to those at home." But Jesus said to him, "No one, after putting his hand to the plow and looking back, is fit for the kingdom of God." (Luke 9:57-62 NASU)

I like how The Message words it in a similar, but unique way.

"On the road someone asked if he could go along. "I'll go with you, wherever," he said. Jesus was curt: "Are you ready to rough it? We're not staying in the best inns, you know." Jesus said to another, "Follow me." He said, "Certainly, but first excuse me for a couple of days, please. I have to make arrangements for my father's funeral." Jesus refused. "First things first. Your business is life, not death. And life is urgent: Announce God's kingdom!"

Then another said, "I'm ready to follow you, Master, but first excuse me while I get things straightened out at home." Jesus said, "No procrastination. No backward looks. You can't put God's kingdom off till tomorrow. Seize the day." (Luke 9:57-62 THE MESSAGE)

(Just one minor side thought to point out before moving on. Jesus said, "We're not staying in the best inns, you know." I wonder how many leaders in the church today would still follow Jesus if they lived as He did? Or walked as He walked? I am sure the numbers would be reduced if such were the case. Maybe they missed it somewhere? And what example are they giving to those who follow them? It doesn't appear to be Yeshua's.)

So my thoughts on this now, to let the dead bury the dead?

I think it is time that we quit sugar-coating the Gospel message, trying to make it fit in today's world, so as not to put too much inconvenience on those needing to hear the Gospel, and repent from living the sinful life. Jesus didn't make it a convenient choice to become His disciple. He spoke right up front to let them know, "This will change your life. What you did yesterday you will no longer do today. The life you led then, it needs to be gone. Repent, take up your cross and follow Me."

Maybe it is time we quit making our Sunday morning a nice place to bring people to, hoping they will receive a "helpful message so you can get saved today", but rather use it as the time to really train Christians to get out into the world to take the Gospel to the dying. For as you may have already realized, they aren't coming to us. We have to go to them. And when we do, we need to tell it the way it is to be.

Let the truth be known. You want to follow Jesus? It will cost you everything you have. You can't have it both ways – to continue living the way you have been six days a week and then "be the Christian" one hour on Sunday. Jesus is requiring a complete lifestyle change. He calls it "repentance". We should too.

Rather then offering a Gospel that allows one to keep doing that which was leading to death anyway, it is time we offered the "radical" Gospel that Jesus did. To all those He came in contact with, He said come, repent, and He would *then* give eternal life in exchange. There cannot be any other way. There has to be a life change through repentance.

"From that time Jesus began to preach and say, "Repent, for the kingdom of heaven is at hand."
(Matthew 4:17 NASU)

He also made it clear that if there was no repentance, there would be no salvation. They would perish in their sin.

"There were present at that season some who told Him about the Galileans whose blood Pilate had mingled with their sacrifices. And Jesus answered and said to them, "Do you suppose that these Galileans were worse sinners than all other Galileans, because they suffered such things? I tell you, no; but unless you repent you will all likewise perish. Or those eighteen on whom the tower in Siloam fell and killed them, do you think that they were worse sinners than all other men who dwelt in Jerusalem? I tell you, no; but unless you repent you will all likewise perish." (Luke 13:1-5 NKJV)

We are called as believers to demonstrate the Kingdom of God in the world around us, by living a life of repentance. We have been called to leave the old life behind, and walk in the new one that Jesus gives us as we do so. And then, the Gospel message is to tell others to do the same. Repent, believe, and follow Jesus. And in that following, they won't be doing the same thing they were doing, with just a slight change. They will be letting go of the old in order to receive the new.

They too will be leaving the dead to bury their own dead. They too will no longer be participating with the things in life that are here today and gone tomorrow. They too will be living the way of the cross, which will eternally bring life.

Just like you and I should be doing ourselves.

3.

A Lighthouse & Watchman

"I am God. I have called you to live right and well. I have taken responsibility for you, kept you safe. I have set you among my people to bind them to me, and provided you as a lighthouse to the nations, to make a start at bringing people into the open, into light: opening blind eyes, releasing prisoners from dungeons, emptying the dark prisons." (Isaiah 42:6-7, THE MESSAGE)

We have been hearing much in our Sunday gatherings on our roles as being watchmen. I take that word seriously, and act on it - to pray, to proclaim, to write accordingly, and then to post on our blog *Love For His People*. Even as the watchman of old sought the Lord, listened to His voice, and spoke out what they were told, I too want to be one who does that.

While being faithful as a watchman to bring the warnings that come with the territory, there is also always hope in the midst of it all, as that comes straight from the Father's heart. His light brought forth, as a lighthouse, guides us through the sea of life.

Jesus' love for the nations causes Him to bring awareness to His people of what is coming. His prophetic words, recorded in the historical Scriptures, both Old and New Testaments, have proven over and over again of His loving actions. The Lord God of Israel, the Messiah, has continually sought to draw us to Himself through those writings, and current warnings.

Another practical, visual way the Lord has also demonstrated His light shining in the world has been through ocean and lakeside lighthouses. Located on many coasts throughout the world yet today, these beacons of light through the centuries have given direction to the incoming vessels, and hope to the ones anxiously watching for a light to guide them safely into the harbor. They have stood tall while withstanding the raging seas and mighty storms that have pounded and battered at their foundations through the years.

Lighthouses are a vivid example of the Lord's hope, standing strong and tall in the battle, shining forth the beam of hope to show us the way.

One summer in the late 90's our family took the time for a vacation trip, to do the eight hours of travel from Charlotte to the Atlantic Coast of North Carolina. Our goal was to visit all seven lighthouses, from Currituck as the northernmost one, stopping at the most famous and tallest Cape Hatteras on the Outer Banks, with the final destination being close to the southern border with South Carolina. We did it in the seven days we had. We started at the northern end, first with **Currituck Beach Light Station, followed by Bodie Island Lighthouse, Cape Hatteras Lighthouse, Ocracoke Lighthouse, Cape Lookout, Oak Island Lighthouse, and finally Old Baldy, on Bald Head Island.** Being that one is only accessible by water or air, we didn't make it out to see it. Someday we may!

As lighthouses and as watchmen too, we have been called upon to stand strong, prepared in our spirits to announce the oncoming storms that seek to take out or overtake the Lord's people. As lighthouses in the spiritual realm, watchmen are to stand ready to shine the light, the silver lining of hope, as the darkness seeks to consume the continents with its encroaching power. The Lord has given us the weapons of warfare and the fortitude established in our character to be the watchmen, and the spiritual lighthouses.

We have been prepared for the war ahead.

4.

Little Things Shared In Love

"…that their hearts may be encouraged, having been knit together in love…"
(Colossians 2:2, NASU)

Just before we were ready to start the conference, my friend and I took a white porcelain stature of a warrior angel, wrapped it in a gift box (as best we could as men), to give it to the ministry administrator. He was in charge of the facility we were renting for our upcoming conference. It was one way we were going to show thanks and appreciation for the effort he had given in helping us with all the details for our three day event held in his building. Remembering what he said still brings a smile to me, as he opened it, held it up, and proclaimed, "I want to thank all the little people who helped me make this possible."

They say it takes a village to raise a child. I believe that is true. Each one offering a bit of themselves to the others, contributing to the greater good of all. As we make our way through life, often it is those little things along the way that encourage us to keep pressing on. The kind word said here, the helping hand given there, the unexpected but so needed support when it seems the road is just too steep to go another step.

The Lord Jesus speaks to us of being faithful in the very little things. When it is all said and done, our showing our faith, by saying that word of encouragement to the discouraged one, will be noted for eternity. Making the effort to visit the weak and lonely, unnoticed by anyone else, may be the one time you kept them living for another day with hope. Even sending a simple thank you card, or a text as today would be the case, can bless another when they need it the most.

Little things done for others along the way can fill up a bucket of love. And when that bucket is full, they too will overflow with more of the same for the next one.

Because the Messiah has first loved us, we can thus give to each other from that wealth of expressed love.

"We, though, are going to love — love and be loved. First we were loved, now we love. He loved us first."
(1 John 4:19, THE MESSAGE)

Little things you do today can make a world of difference in others needing a touch from the Lord in this hour. Look around. Find that one. And do even a little thing to bring a smile to their face.

Amazing love shared will do your heart good too.

"Ahava" in Hebrew – located in Israel National Park.
"Love" in English.

5.

When It Hasn't Happened Yet

"My soul, wait in silence for God alone, because my hope comes from him. He alone is my rock and salvation, my stronghold; I won't be moved." (Psalm 62:6-7 Complete Jewish Bible)

Disappointment and discouragement go hand in hand. You had put your hopes on an expected desire to be fulfilled, and it didn't happen. Discouragement then followed, and you even wondered if what had been promised to you would ever happen. It has been two years, five years, even seven years since the word was delivered to you. Might it even be 40? What is going on Lord?

Thinking back, you believe you did all the right things along the way. You prayed, you fasted, you gave yourself to everything you knew to do. And yet in the time you thought it would have come by now it had not. The right person to marry, that move to another location to start over, the beginning of a new work that had been burning in your heart since youth.

"Surely this was you Lord, and yet when will it come to pass? Why is it taking so long?" you cry silently in your heart.

We all know the stories of Moses and Joseph, who each were given a word that they would do something great for God. For Moses, it was to lead God's people out of the long-endured suffering in Egypt. For Joseph, it was to rule a nation in order to save his family, and many others. Both of these would be mighty accomplishments if they ever happened. But years into the struggle to believe, it hadn't. I can imagine Moses (Moshe in Hebrew) saying to himself in the 39th year, "I am quitting. This will never happen. How could I have been so wrong?"

And Joseph, in prison for two years, previously spending 11 with the Egyptian Potiphar after being bought as his slave, could have said the same. "It won't happen. The dream was just a dream. What was I thinking?"

How many times have we come so close to seeing something completed, a dream come true, and then we gave up hope just short of it? Probably more that we would know, by not allowing the Lord's time period to be completed. But even in those times we missed it, the Lord was still directing our steps. He realizes our weaknesses, and accomplishes His will in spite of those shortcomings.

Knowing that our Lord Jesus knows all, I am encouraged that He will indeed finish what He started. The hope within, to keep on pressing on, even when it seems nothing will change, in and of itself is a gift from the Lord. His Holy Spirit within us is there to help us keep believing, trusting, and seeing our dream accomplished. After all, He is the One who gave us the dream. And when it hasn't happened as yet, He will give us the grace and fortitude to keep hoping and trusting until it does.

I encourage you to keep your eyes fixed on Jesus, the Author and Finisher of your faith.

"Therefore we also, since we are surrounded by so great a cloud of witnesses, let us lay aside every weight, and the sin which so easily ensnares us, and let us run with endurance the race that is set before us, 2 looking unto Jesus, the author and finisher of our faith, who for the joy that was set before Him endured the cross, despising the shame, and has sat down at the right hand of the throne of God." (Hebrews 12:1-2, NKJV)

The promise, the dream, the desire of your heart will come to pass. The Lord Himself gave that to you, and He was not kidding around. What He says He will do, He will do. Keep strong in your faith, and don't give up.

Clock received by Steve Martin.

"From Derek Prince Ministries Over 7 yrs Faithful Service" 2010

6.

Soft & Tender

"Because your heart was tender and you humbled yourself before God when you heard His words against this place and against its inhabitants, and because you humbled yourself before Me, tore your clothes and wept before Me, I truly have heard you," declares the Lord."
(2 Chronicles 34:27-28 NASU)

When I heard the Lord speak the word "soft" while I slept, I knew it was from Him. But then that was it. Just the word "soft". What did that mean, and what would He have me write about it?

When I got out of bed about two hours later, I remembered the word I had heard. As I normally do in times when I am given a word, I asked the Lord to further explain what it meant. So I prayed in tongues, read some Scripture, and did a concordance search for the word "soft". Surprisingly, when I went to my Bible software program on my computer, I realized the name of it was *PC Study Bible V5*, by *BibleSoft*. I have used this program for over six years, and had never really thought about the developer's name. But I was getting somewhere.

The Lord Jesus (Yeshua) likes to do that. He gives you something, whether it is just a word, a picture in your mind, or what you might think of as just another "random thought", which can typically be from the Holy Spirit, to see what you will do with it. He is wanting you to seek Him further, to dig deeper into your relationship with Him. As we pursue the Lord and His kingdom, He will show Himself more to us, and what are the plans and purposes in His heart, for you and the nations.

"It is the glory of God to conceal a matter, but the glory of kings is to search out a matter." (Proverbs 25:2, NASU)

So what did I find in my "gold digging" treasure hunt?

After doing a search on just the word "soft" in the Bible program, the verses that came up with that word in them didn't really speak anything that I would think He was wanting to say. So I asked the Holy Spirit to further bring clarity, and the word "tender" came to mind. So I did a search on that word.

And this was one Scripture that did stand out above the others.

"But to the king of Judah who sent you to inquire of the Lord, thus you will say to him, 'Thus says the Lord God of Israel regarding the words which you have heard, "Because your heart was *tender* and you humbled yourself before God when you heard His words against this place and against its inhabitants, and because you humbled yourself before Me, tore your clothes and wept before Me, I truly have heard you," declares the Lord." (2 Chronicles 34:26-28 NASU)

In these dark times we are living in, when evil seems to be encroaching in every sacred area we have held dear, our own hearts can become hardened to people. Rather than praying for mercy and grace in their lives for repentance, I know personally sometimes for me my request to the Lord is to just send judgment and get it all over with. Enough already with the filth and wickedness.

But to know the Father's heart in these times, I am the one who needs to humble myself before the Lord and continue to cry out for mercy for them and our nation. His heart is not for me to call down fire and brimstone, but to intercede on their behalf. That isn't always easy to do. But it is the right thing to do, while leaving the judgment times in the Lord's hands.

Because the Lord is a holy God, the days are coming when He will judge the nations for their wickedness and ungodly acts. That is truly written in His word. But until that day comes, my attitude and heart is to keep praying for my co-workers and neighbors who'd rather seek pleasure and wealth than the living God of Israel, to order to walk in His ways.

"Keep my heart soft and tender for Your ways O Lord" must be among my prayers. "Let me not give up in seeking Your face for the nations, until the time comes when You act according to Your Word."

Together we can have the heart of the loving Father, and see more of the unsaved come into the salvation found only in His Son Jesus. His Kingdom will come when we do according to His will.

7.

I Want It

"But thanks be to God, who always leads us in triumph in Christ, and manifests through us the sweet aroma of the knowledge of Him in every place. For we are a fragrance of Christ to God among those who are being saved and among those who are perishing; to the one an aroma from death to death, to the other an aroma from life to life." (2 Corinthians 2:14-16, NASU)

Have you ever stopped and realized that when you see someone with something you don't have, one first instinct is to say, "I want it."

It could be anything, such as a new house (or one newer than what you have now), a better car, a more likeable job, or just a day with no problems to contend with. I noticed myself "wanting it" when I was looking out an office lobby window at lunch time and saw several people on the sidewalk carrying orange plastic bags. They looked like they had been at a convention uptown. All carried the orange bag. My first thought was, "I want one."

Wow, another bag. As if I really needed one.

Is it just our human nature to want something that another has and we don't? I think so. Look at Jacob and Esau, for instance. It was during the time of the patriarchs when Jacob wanted Esau's birthright and he schemed, along with his mother, to get it. Or go back further in history's timeline, to that Scripture telling of Cain and Abel. Cain wanted the Lord's approval for his crop sacrifice, which was not what the Lord was requiring. A blood sacrifice was needed to be acceptable, as Abel had provided with his lamb. (This was a foreshadow of the Messiah Jesus', Yeshua HaMashiach's, sacrificial blood poured out on the cross. The sacrifice God required could not be satisfied with something obtained from our own human efforts and toil, as was Cain's presentation. It had to be a blood sacrifice provided by the Lord Himself.)

Jacob and Cain each wanted what his brother had. They were jealous that the other possessed it, and thus wanted it for themselves.

Looking at it from the other side, as I work with co-workers who do not follow after the Lord, I find myself at times checking what I am presenting to them, as a believer in the Lord Jesus. Is my life's testimony something they would want for themselves? Do they see or sense His Holy Spirit in my life, and desire Him, even if they may not realize Who He is?

Many days I think not. In my mind, sometimes my testimony is not what I would like it to be "on the job". Those days when I struggle with life's issues, my thought is that I am not portraying the "victorious" life that I believe we are to be sharing with others. (And yet even of those times I choose not to walk under the enemy's condemnation because of it.) Those surrounding me may even realize that life as a believer on this earth isn't a bed of roses, which some were led to believe it would be at that initial salvation experience. But we press on in the midst of our struggles, with His grace working within us always.

When I think my testimony isn't the greatest, the Lord still encourages me. He reminds me of those people who have let me know, after I left a particularly place of employment, how my presence there had made a difference. They were watching me in my day to day activities, knowing what I stood for, and how I handled most situations. A seed had been planted in their heart and spirit. They knew there was something more than just the life they had. My prayer now for them is that another believer will water that seed, and it will blossom in due time.

As the dark gets darker, the light we have, the Holy Spirit shining within us, will be bright and illuminate more than we would imagine. Even as a single match lights up a pitch black room, so we will be that to others in these times we live in.

My prayer is that those ones around us will be saying to themselves at some point, "I want it. Whatever they got, I want it in my life." And then may the Lord Jesus come and reveal Himself to them, having used us as part of His plan fulfilled.

"For we are a fragrance of Christ to God among those who are being saved and among those who are perishing; to the one an aroma from death to death, to the other an aroma from life to life."

8.

Tilt Your Head Up

"I will lift up my eyes to the hills — from whence comes my help? My help comes from the Lord, Who made heaven and earth." (Psalm 121:1-2 NKJV)

"Tilt your head up", I heard the Voice softly say as I prayed.

As one normally does, I had my head bowed during my morning prayers, as I sat in my prayer chair in the corner of our home's front room. I don't recall that I was praying for anything real heavy at the time. But when He spoke, I also had the sensation of a father touching the chin of their child with their fingers, to lift their head in order to see into their eyes.

The Lord was telling me to look up; to see Him; to know that He was in full control.

"He will not allow your foot to be moved; He who keeps you will not slumber. Behold, He who keeps Israel shall neither slumber nor sleep. The Lord is your keeper; the Lord is your shade at your right hand. The sun shall not strike you by day, nor the moon by night. The Lord shall preserve you from all evil; He shall preserve your soul. The Lord shall preserve your going out and your coming in from this time forth, and even forevermore." (Psalm 121:3-8 NKJV)

The Lord's loving-kindness and compassion to us are new every morning, as Scripture tells us. His faithfulness, to hear every prayer, and to speak to our heart, is a promise for those who take the time to seek Him. Therefore we can have hope and trust in Him.

"The Lord's lovingkindnesses indeed never cease, for His compassions never fail. They are new every morning; great is Your faithfulness. "The Lord is my portion," says my soul, "Therefore I have hope in Him." The Lord is good to those who wait for Him, to the person who seeks Him. It is good that he waits silently for the salvation of the Lord." (Lam 3:22-26, NASU)

We can easily get weighted down with the daily cares of the world. The day in, day out routine, which can be a grind at times, fills our soul with anxiety. We simply get worn out. That is one of the strategies of the enemy that opposes us. If we don't stop and let the Lord Jesus' yoke become ours, we will be overcome by it all.

Daily prayer, with reading of the Bible, isn't an option we can pick or chose when we want to, or feel like it. It has to be so normal in our normal lives that when we miss the time with Him, we know that we have missed it. May it be that our day will not be the same without time with Him.

I encourage you to make prayer and the reading of His Word a priority in your life. If it means going to bed a little earlier, so you can have that quiet time in the morning before the rush is on, then do it. Or if you are better at night, after things quiet down, then spend this time with the Lord then. Let Him know that He is a priority in your life. And as for you, you will be more aware of how you are a priority in His.

He wants to tilt your head up to Him, to look into His eyes, and know that He is in control.

The Lord cares all about us. He cares for our spirit, He cares for our body, He cares for our soul. He even cares about our lost keys. If we seek Him, He will show us the way.

I bless the Lord and will daily call upon His Name. He is our salvation, which is the meaning of His Name, Yeshua (Jesus) in Hebrew. Thank you Lord!

9.

Held By Your Love Lord

"For I am convinced that neither death nor life, neither angels nor other heavenly rulers, neither what exists nor what is coming, neither powers above nor powers below, nor any other created thing will be able to separate us from the love of God which comes to us through the Messiah Yeshua, our Lord." (Romans 8:38-39, Complete Jewish Bible)

There was a time, with so many great memories, when I was completely inspired by Integrity Music's Hosanna! Music series. Every other month, beginning in 1987, they came out with a worship cassette (and then it was CDs) with music that just captured my heart, and my listening ear, every time. As many of you may have done yourself at times, like I did with these, you would wear out your favorite cassette, just by playing it over and over again. (But now with MP3, that won't happen!)

In 2001 Integrity published a CD by Bob Fitts, a worship leader whom I had heard before, on previous albums. This one was entitled ***I Will Bow To You***. The 11th song was "I'm Held By Your Love", written by Karen Lim. For this song Bob is joined by his wife Kathy as they sang it live at their home church, New Creation Church, in Singapore. What an amazing song! (The lyrics can be found below, and a link to the song itself is added, so you can listen to it on our ministry blog.)

The opening verse clearly speaks of our Lord's love for us. If ever you have doubted this, just keep listening over and over to these words, and let them swell up in your heart.

I'm held by Your love, upheld by Your strength. On your shoulders You bore me, by Your faith I stand. Cherished by You Lord, treasured in Your sight, so close to Your heart, held firm in Your hand."

Every now and then, more now than "then", you need to be reminded of the simple fact that our Lord Jesus, Yeshua the Messiah, loves you more than you can comprehend. The very fact that He came, lived the life on earth to be as us, suffered a cruel torture, was crucified in death, and then rose again from the grave that could never hold Him, to prove that He alone is the Awesome God we serve. Because of that historical fact, we can know His love for us will be eternally upheld.

"By entering through faith into what God has always wanted to do for us — set us right with him, make us fit for him — we have it all together with God because of our Master Jesus. And that's not all: We throw open our doors to God and discover at the same moment that he has already thrown open his door to us. We find ourselves standing where we always hoped we might stand — out in the wide open spaces of God's grace and glory, standing tall and shouting our praise.

There's more to come: We continue to shout our praise even when we're hemmed in with troubles, because we know how troubles can develop passionate patience in us, and how that patience in turn forges the tempered steel of virtue, keeping us alert for whatever God will do next. In alert expectancy such as this, we're never left feeling shortchanged. Quite the contrary — we can't round up enough containers to hold everything God generously pours into our lives through the Holy Spirit!

Christ arrives right on time to make this happen. He didn't, and doesn't, wait for us to get ready. He presented himself for this sacrificial death when we were far too weak and rebellious to do anything to get ourselves ready. And even if we hadn't been so weak, we wouldn't have known what to do anyway. We can understand someone dying for a person worth dying for, and we can understand how someone good and noble could inspire us to selfless sacrifice. But God put his love on the line for us by offering his Son in sacrificial death while we were of no use whatever to him.

Now that we are set right with God by means of this sacrificial death, the consummate blood sacrifice, there is no longer a question of being at odds with God in any way. If, when we were at our worst, we were put on friendly terms with God by the sacrificial death of his Son, now that we're at our best, just think of how our lives will expand and deepen by means of his resurrection life! Now that we have actually received this amazing friendship with God, we are no longer content to simply say it in plodding prose. We sing and shout our praises to God through Jesus, the Messiah!" (Romans 5:1-11, THE MESSAGE)

Drawing near to Him, in quiet meditation and a time set apart to experience this love, will enable you to experience His strength, goodness, and lovingkindness daily in your walk with Him.

Read the lyrics. Listen to the song. Let the love of the Father draw you close to Him.

10.

Silence is Golden

"Let the words of my mouth and the meditation of my heart be acceptable in Your sight,
O Lord, my rock and my Redeemer." (Psalms 19:14 NASU)

Have you ever caught yourself thinking about something, and then wonder how you got to that point in your mind? Day dreaming about tomorrow? Pondering over a situation that has nothing to do with what you are doing now?

If you then catch yourself doing that, and next try to walk back to how you got there in your thinking, it can be as a maze in your mind. It is probably due to the fact that our minds have collected so much information over the years. No wonder we wander.

In years gone by I would memorize Scripture, to help my mind be disciplined. I would meditate on good things. The shepherd David learned this lesson, as he sat watching over the sheep grazing. I can imagine that gave him plenty of time to consider what he allowed in his mind, and he made sure it was good.

How often do we surround ourselves with the radio blaring continually, the TV turned on with meaningless content, or the overflowing noise of life which distracts us from the Lord? Far too often I am sure. How can we meditate on His Words if all else consumes our minds?

Many times we avoid having it quiet. It is like we can't allow "nothing" in the airwaves around us. We have become so accustomed to noise that if there isn't any we look to have something turned on to make it. Ever walk into a hotel room and immediately turn on the TV? (Guilty!)

It is almost like we fear having a quiet time. Something has to be going all the time, or we tend to get paranoid. Does that describe you?

There was a song written decades ago with the lyrics "silence is golden."* Do you believe that?

The Lord isn't calling us to be as hermits living in a secluded cave in the desert land of some far away country. Nor are most of us supposed to join the monastery to live as a monk, or nun, where talk is prohibited 23 hours a day. But I do think He is asking us to allow His Holy Spirit to have time to speak to us, when we are able to hear Him. Most of the time He will be that "still, small voice" which can only be heard when nothing else is filling our ears, or minds.

Elijah was given a lesson in listening. Scripture records this about him.

"Then He said, "Go out, and stand on the mountain before the Lord." And behold, the Lord passed by, and a great and strong wind tore into the mountains and broke the rocks in pieces before the Lord, but the Lord was not in the wind; and after the wind an earthquake, but the Lord was not in the earthquake; and after the earthquake a fire, but the Lord was not in the fire; and after the fire a still small voice.

"So it was, when Elijah heard it, that he wrapped his face in his mantle and went out and stood in the entrance of the cave. Suddenly a voice came to him, and said, "What are you doing here, Elijah?" And he said, "I have been very zealous for the Lord God of hosts; because the children of Israel have forsaken Your covenant, torn down Your altars, and killed Your prophets with the sword. I alone am left; and they seek to take my life."

Then the Lord said to him: "Go, return on your way to the Wilderness of Damascus; and when you arrive, anoint Hazael as king over Syria. Also you shall anoint Jehu the son of Nimshi as king over Israel. And Elisha the son of Shaphat of Abel Meholah you shall anoint as prophet in your place. It shall be that whoever escapes the sword of Hazael, Jehu will kill; and whoever escapes the sword of Jehu, Elisha will kill. Yet I have reserved seven thousand in Israel, all whose knees have not bowed to Baal, and every mouth that has not kissed him." (1 Kings 19:11-18, NKJV)

It is amazing what we can hear when we give the Lord the opportunity to speak. For Elijah, that meant receiving instruction to go and anoint the next king of Syria. And Israel. And also the next prophet who would take his place. Wow!

Are you afraid of what the Lord will tell you today, if you give Him time to speak a word to you during a quiet time? Personally, I long to hear the Lord speak. My life history tells me it will be for good, as I have learned it to be. His next word just may change my life's direction, or simply give me the next step on the path I need to walk on. That could be the same for you today too.

Seek the Lord and He will be found. Call upon His Name and He will answer you. Both promises that will eternally hold true. Even now.

A blessed person will make it a priority each day to give time for the Lord and His Spirit to speak.

11.

What If...There Was No Resurrection?

"But if there is no resurrection of the dead, not even Christ has been raised; and if Christ has not been raised, then our preaching is vain, your faith also is vain." 1 Corinthians 15:13-15 NASU)

What if...there was no resurrection, and Jesus' body decayed in the tomb, just like everyone else who died?

What if, when Miriam came to anoint Yeshua's body with spices, as was common, that He was still there? And later His bones were found in an ossuary?

What if it really was a hoax, as the Temple priests wanted the world to believe, and the word spread about the disciples hiding His body so they could say that Jesus had been resurrected from the dead, was true?

If it were so, and there was no resurrection on the third day as Jesus had prophesied, then...

...the 12 disciples were complete fools in traveling the world, telling He was alive, and then martyred for nothing.

…Saul from Tarsus saw someone, or something, other than the resurrected Lord, on his way to Damascus to kill believers, and then too was completely mistaken for all his believing years, speaking a false Gospel of hope throughout the Roman Empire.

Years after his encounter of the Lord on that day, he wrote to the Corinthians, describing how not only would their faith be in vain, but "Moreover we are even found to be false witnesses of God, because we testified against God that He raised Christ, whom He did not raise, if in fact the dead are not raised. For if the dead are not raised, not even Christ has been raised; and if Christ has not been raised, your faith is worthless; you are still in your sins. Then those also who have fallen asleep in Christ have perished. If we have hoped in Christ in this life only, we are of all men most to be pitied." (1 Corinthians 15:15-19, NASU)

If the resurrection were not so, then "we are of all men most to be pitied."

What if there were no resurrection?

Then all the men and women through the centuries, who perished by sword, fire, rocks, arrows or bullets, who had proclaimed the death, burial and resurrection of Jesus Christ, would not be in heaven, but rather now suffer in eternal hell with all the other non-believers through the ages.

If Jesus had not been raised from the dead, what are we doing, looking to salvation from our sins, if the Perfect Sacrifice had not happened? What hope do we ourselves have for eternity?

"But the fact is that the Messiah has been raised from the dead, the firstfruits of those who have died. For since death came through a man, also the resurrection of the dead has come through a man." (1 Corinthians 15:20-22 Complete Jewish Bible)

This had been predicted by the Jewish prophets centuries before, that the Messiah would come, and be the One to fulfill the Hope of Israel.

From Isaiah 53:1-12:

"Who has believed our message?
And to whom has the arm of the Lord been revealed?
For He grew up before Him like a tender shoot,
And like a root out of parched ground;
He has no stately form or majesty
That we should look upon Him,
Nor appearance that we should be attracted to Him.

He was despised and forsaken of men,
A man of sorrows and acquainted with grief;
And like one from whom men hide their face
He was despised, and we did not esteem Him.

Surely our griefs He Himself bore,
And our sorrows He carried;
Yet we ourselves esteemed Him stricken,

Smitten of God, and afflicted.

But He was pierced through for our transgressions,
He was crushed for our iniquities;
The chastening for our well-being fell upon Him,

All of us like sheep have gone astray,
Each of us has turned to his own way;
But the Lord has caused the iniquity of us all
To fall on Him.

He was oppressed and He was afflicted,
Yet He did not open His mouth;
 Like a lamb that is led to slaughter,
And like a sheep that is silent before its shearers,
So He did not open His mouth.

By oppression and judgment He was taken away;
And as for His generation, who considered
That He was cut off out of the land of the living
 For the transgression of my people, to whom the stroke was due?

His grave was assigned with wicked men,
Yet He was with a rich man in His death,
 Because He had done no violence,
Nor was there any deceit in His mouth.

But the Lord was pleased
To crush Him, putting Him to grief;
If He would render Himself as a guilt offering,
He will see His offspring,
He will prolong His days,

And the good pleasure of the Lord will prosper in His hand.

As a result of the anguish of His soul,
He will see it and be satisfied;
By His knowledge the Righteous One,
My Servant, will justify the many,
As He will bear their iniquities.

Therefore, I will allot Him a portion with the great,
And He will divide the booty with the strong;
Because He poured out Himself to death,
And was numbered with the transgressors;
Yet He Himself bore the sin of many,
And interceded for the transgressors."

Because His grave is empty and indeed the resurrection did take place, our faith is on solid ground, and will stand come what may. The testimony of millions, from the first century through today, will ever proclaim that Jesus Christ lives and continues to save the hearts and souls of mankind. Your trust in Him is yet another fact that the world can see to believe also.

The "what if" became the "fact is", with Jesus being the solid rock to stand on. Truth will always win out in the end.

12.

Take the Time

"Seek the Lord and His strength; Seek His face continually." Psalm 105:4 NASU)

How common it is for us to get into the car and turn the radio or CD on. Listen to some music. Catch the latest news. Drown out the work thoughts so you can leave them behind on the commute home.

It used to be an automatic thing for me. Once the car had started, I would reach over and push the knob on. The noise was there.

But then the Lord would ask me, "Do you want to spend some time with Me on the way home?" When I first heard that question months ago, I had the guilt trip of wanting time to myself, and do what I wanted to do. But then I realized He wanted to have some time with me; not take away my "own" time.

After the learning incident, I now ask before I just go into auto pilot and switch on the radio. "Anything you'd like to talk about, Lord?" Sometimes I also realize that He just wants to train my mind to take a break, and not feel the necessity to always have something going on. I am learning that more often than we think our Lord is wanting to teach us the importance of experiencing quiet, or allow Him to speak to us, if we take the time.

Have you ever thought why it is that some prisoners come to the Lord while incarcerated? It may be because they are finally in a place where things stop moving all around them, or in particular themselves, and they have that quiet time, undisturbed by outside stimulus. He has them in a place where they can finally listen.

Similarly, I know people who have gotten sick, and would later tell me, "God had to slow me down so He could speak to me."

Maybe we can initiate the time ourselves, before the Lord would have to allow a sickness, or even imprisonment in some cases, to get our attention? But it seems history proves otherwise. The Lord will get our attention, using any means He desires, for our own good in the long run.

Keeping this message short will give you time to stop, listen, and acknowledge His desire to speak to you. That will be a good thing for you.

13.

Steps Along the Way

"Your word is a lamp to my feet and a light to my path." Psalm 119:105 NASU)

At some of the most unexpected, but most needed times, the Lord sends a word of encouragement along the way. During those times when we are uncertain, unclear, or unknowing which next step to take, the Lord will bring a word to encourage us to keep walking.

It seems that being faithful in obedience requires us to do that which we know to do when we know we must continue doing it. Especially when the light isn't as bright as we'd like, we must keep walking in the light we know. We must be steadfast in our convictions and hold the ground we have been called to stand on.

Because the Lord is faithful, He may not always give us a full powered flashlight or ocean lighthouse to show us the way, but He will shine a light on the path ahead of us to show the way to go. He will also give us a word, from His Holy Word, through a friend's word of encouragement, or by His Holy Spirit breathing a remembrance of something we heard as a promise years ago, and really need to hear again at this moment in time.

Walking the walk will cause us to be mindful of keeping our eyes upon Jesus, the Author and the Finisher of our faith. To keep us from stumbling along the way, due to rocks, roots, or other obstacles, natural and spiritual, our hearts must be strong in Him, relying on His light of encouragement and direction as we step along the way.

We all need an encouraging word now and then, reminding us of the way we are to go, to keep on going. I am thankful to You, Lord, that You have walked this walk, and know exactly what we need, when we need it most.

14.

Faithful

"He was faithful to Him who appointed Him, as Moses also was in all His house.
(Hebrews 3:2-3, NASU)

Faithful. Now that is a word we don't hear enough of these days when describing another, or when someone describes ourselves.

How often have you heard it being said of one, "He was faithful to his wife." Or, "She kept her promises. If she said it, you can be sure she would do it. She was faithful to the end."

So often we hear of the politician who said one thing before the election day, but once in office they seemed to have forgotten what they had spoken, and instead bend to the peer pressure surrounding them. Or the sad stories reported of school teachers taking advantage of their students, having sex with them, unfaithful both to their student and their commitment to teach truth.

It has been far too often that leadership has failed us. Out of their mouth has come one thing, but behind the scene it is discovered that unfaithfulness to their God and the people they were called to serve was the opposite of what picture was painted for the world to see. Disappointment may then come upon their followers, which then cause them to give up believing in anyone trustworthy. A cynical spirit is thus given a place to lodge in people's hearts.

We have been called to be a witness of the Lord Jesus. He Who was faithful to the end, during His time on earth, and for all eternity, has too chosen and appointed us to be as He is – faithful and true.

"Thus says the Lord,
The Redeemer of Israel, their Holy One,
To Him whom man despises,
To Him whom the nation abhors,
To the Servant of rulers:
"Kings shall see and arise,
Princes also shall worship,
Because of the Lord who is faithful,
The Holy One of Israel;
And He has chosen You." Isaiah 49:7 NKJV

Our lives, demonstrated before the world, are to be ones proving the faithfulness of the One we serve. If we say we are going to do something, we must do it. If we commit to be there when we say we will, then we must be there. On time and ready for action.

The desire of the Lord's child must be to someday hear Him speak to them the word He spoke in parable, "His lord said to him, 'Well done, good and faithful servant; you were faithful over a few things, I will make you ruler over many things. Enter into the joy of your lord.'" (Matthew 25:21-22 NKJV)

May it be said of us in our days that we are faithful, that we do what we will say we will do; that we keep our promises, no matter what the cost is to ourselves. May others say of us today, "They are faithful." And may our God say of us when we stand before Him on that day, "You are a good and faithful servant. Enter into the joy of your Lord."

15.

Israel & Our Friends

"He has said, "It is not enough that you are merely my servant to raise up the tribes of Ya'akov and restore the offspring of Isra'el. I will also make you a light to the nations, so my salvation can spread to the ends of the earth." (Isaiah 49:6, Complete Jewish Bible)

In a few days Laurie and I will embark on another overseas trip to spend time with our friends in Israel. This will be my 12th journey to the Land. For Laurie, her third. As part of the ministry of *Love For His People*, founded by us in 2010, we seek to show further tangible support for those we lift up in our prayers, with our voice, and with ongoing monthly financial blessing. We spend time with families similar to yours and ours, demonstrating our solid commitment to stand strong with them.

It is a spiritual connection, supernatural in design, bestowed by the Lord Himself. As Derek Prince once said, "You don't choose Jerusalem; Jerusalem chooses you." In other words, the Lord God of Israel is the One who speaks His words, choosing ones to stand in the spiritual battle realm, supporting those He has called as His chosen ones. And as a debt we owe to the Jewish people, we take our stand alongside them.

Over the centuries the Jews have been the faithful ones to receive and write down His Scriptures, carefully and dutifully passing them to the next generations, as His Holy Spirit spoke the anointed words through the Jewish prophets. And at the proper time, in fulfillment of the prophecies, the Messiah Yeshua (Jesus), came as promised for the good of the nations. If it had not been for their diligence, endurance and commitment through those centuries of destruction, murder and banishment throughout the nations, believers would not have the roots of our faith today.

In the last 100 years and more, the Lord has been regathering the Jews from all over the world to this land promised to them, given in covenant specifically to them since the days of Abraham and Moses. To be a light to the nations, demonstrating the eternal love of God the Father, together with His Only Son, they are fulfilling that prophetic word. Because of His protection and faithfulness to them, this will ever be their home.

"'He who scattered Israel will gather him, and keep him as a shepherd does his flock.' (Jeremiah 31:10, NKJV)

"Let all the earth fear the Lord; let all the inhabitants of the world stand in awe of Him. For He spoke, and it was done; He commanded, and it stood fast. The Lord nullifies the counsel of the nations; He frustrates the plans of the peoples. The counsel of the Lord stands forever, the plans of His heart from generation to generation.

Blessed is the nation whose God is the Lord, the people whom He has chosen for His own inheritance." (Psalm 33:8-12, NASU)

We delight to uphold the Lord's plans for His people. We count it a joy to be a part of His purposes for Israel in these last days. We continue to give ourselves to strengthen, encourage and freely give to those who have stood for Him.

To the believers in Yeshua, we give thanks for their commitment to His Name. For those who are yet to know the Messiah, we say that your time will come, and we will be there for you.

16.

Being Faithful

"Preserve my life, for I am faithful; save your servant, who puts his trust in you because you are my God." (Psalm 86:2, Complete Jewish Bible)

Ever feel like being faithful is tough? I guess if it wasn't, then everyone would be faithful. Just by looking around you can easily see that that isn't happening.

There are days when being faithful can be real weary. Often we are going upstream, as the world flows in the opposite direction. That in and of itself makes us worn out often. We are tempted to back off, back down, or let it go. Standing for what is right, resisting the ungodly ways of the people, in and of itself tends to drag us down. But we must continue to be faithful to the Lord and His ways.

King David prayed often for strength - to resist the enemy, to achieve victory, and to be an overcomer. He continually put his trust in the Lord, declaring to himself and others that the God of Israel was his God. Therefore his trust placed in the right direction, upward, enabled him to be the faithful servant that he was. He had learned through the temptations, trials and circumstances that God was faithful; therefore his trust in Him would bring the ability for himself to be faithful.

Doing the daily tasks we are called to do requires us to keep pressing on. The repeated jobs, day after day, can seem mundane and purposeless sometimes, especially if we see no movement forward in our lives. Caring for children, maintaining a household, showing up every day for the assigned work - week in and week out – bring constant pressures and stress, working on our minds, bodies and spirits. If it wasn't for the grace of the Lord Jesus, we would end up overdosed, over drugged, and over worked, even as the masses already are. Therefore we must constantly keep our eyes and hearts fixed on Him, as it says in Hebrews.

"…fixing our eyes on Jesus, the author and perfecter of faith, who for the joy set before Him endured the cross, despising the shame, and has sat down at the right hand of the throne of God. For consider Him who has endured such hostility by sinners against Himself, so that you will not grow weary and lose heart." (Hebrews 12:2-3 NASU)

Be encouraged that you will make it, you will be rewarded, and you will see the Lord's end purposes as you continue to be faithful in your daily walk. We are on the winning side.

17.

Cycles

"A man has joy by the answer of his mouth, and a word spoken in due season, how good it is!" (Proverbs 15:23, NKJV)

All around us there are cycles. The nightly sky typically glows with the light of the moon, which completes a full cycle from a new moon to a full moon in 29.5 days. The Hebrew or Jewish calendar is based on this, these lunisolar phases, giving the Jews a consistent basis for anticipating feasts and regular days of consistent life.

New years come and go. We count on them to bring the completion of one year, bringing hope for a better one to come, and maybe start over in certain aspects in our lives. According to the Julian calendar, every 365 days that specific cycle comes full circle.

"You made the moon to mark the seasons, and the sun knows when to set. You bring darkness, and it is night, the time when all forest animals prowl. The young lions roar after their prey and seek their food from God. The sun rises, they slink away and lie down to rest in their dens; while people go out to their work, laboring on till evening.

What variety there is in your works, Adonai! How many [of them there are]! In wisdom you have made them all; the earth is full of your creations. (Psalm 104:19-24 Complete Jewish Bible)

In most climates of the earth, we have the four seasons. Spring, summer, fall and winter bring new life, new growth and new creation before the annual cycle completes its life with "death" or hibernation settling in for months, before it starts all over again. For many, this continual cycle is very refreshing, bringing the newness of flourishing green, yellow, red, and all colors of the rainbow in vegetation and bird life, as the cycle repeats itself.

Certainly our God is a God of cycles. With so many examples in the natural, we can expect to find them also in the spiritual.

"However, the spiritual is not first, but the natural; then the spiritual. The first man is from the earth, earthy; the second man is from heaven. As is the earthy, so also are those who are earthy; and as is the heavenly, so also are those who are heavenly. Just as we have borne the image of the earthy, we will also bear the image of the heavenly." 1 Corinthians 15:46-49 NASU)

Often I have been amazed at these spiritual cycles. I have written of them over my years, and can clearly see seven year markers on this life timeline. I can go back in my spiritual walk and map the years based on these seven year increments, seeing major highlights and milestones that the Lord Jesus had established and planned through them, believing they were assigned even before my birth.

"Before I formed you in the womb I knew you, and before you were born I consecrated you; I have appointed you a prophet to the nations." (Jeremiah 1:5, NASU)

At times I need to remind myself of these cycles, believing that even while I am yet in the middle of another one, finding myself once again wondering if the completion of expectations will yet come soon, that the past promises fulfilled can be a foretelling proof of the future ones also being prophetically fulfilled. In the proper time of course.

You too can count on the Almighty God to bring completion of cycles in your life. Whether you are in the beginning, middle or end of your current spiritual one, the hope placed within can see you through to the circle being completed, with new life brought forth once again. As we keep our eyes on the Lord, our Eternal Hope, Author and Finisher of our faith, certainly we can stand on solid ground, and see dreams and visions come to fruition. In His time it shall be so.

Be glad that the Creator of all, Who has set in motion consistent cycles in your natural and spiritual life, will surely come through once again in your life through these spiritual cycles. We can count on Him to do it. He is Faithful and True.

Persevere to the end. You will see the cycle's completion and rejoice in His love, wisdom and provision.

**Steve & Laurie Martin
Israel 2016**

18.

Dogs

"Then God said, "Let the earth bring forth living creatures after their kind: cattle and creeping things and beasts of the earth after their kind"; and it was so. God made the beasts of the earth after their kind, and the cattle after their kind, and everything that creeps on the ground after its kind; and God saw that it was good." (Genesis 1:24-25, NKJV)

For a long time I considered writing about dogs, but didn't think it would be a good *Now Think On This* message. My thought was, "Why would the Lord have me write about dogs?" But now I feel so led. (Sorry cat lovers. I probably will never write about cats. Just not my cup of tea.)

Because I believe the Lord will have us enjoy His creation of creatures also in heaven, how appropriate that we can share that love for them while on this earth. After all, He created them even before He created mankind, so it wasn't an afterthought of His. All of His creation of birds, fish, reptiles and mammals are quite a feat. But it seems that dogs have been especially helpful, loyal, and the favorite of most people.

For a long time our family did not have a dog. A few stray cats had made their way into our lives over the years (for the kids' sake, not mine) and even a white rabbit was a wholesome pet. Finally, ten years ago, as a fulfillment of a promise I had made to my good wife Laurie, our Dachshund Zoe was the hit Christmas present of the year. She remains a joy in our home yet today – a few inches longer and a lot of pounds heavier.

I am fascinated by dogs. As I watch them in their daily motions, one of which is how they respond when seeing a friend or family member, it brings delight. With the tail wagging, the eyes lit up, and even a playful bark in greeting, their expression of love does the spirit good. Even the wet licks of love, another kind showing of affection, keeps spreading more of their own joy to the other.

One can learn patience from them. Waiting at the front door for the home arrival of the family member, it seems that time does not deter them as the clock ticks by. They will wait as long as it takes.

They are content with the simple things they have – a favorite toy chased after during playtime; a tossed bone after the dinner table is cleared; a treat given to them once they have returned from the morning outing. For some it is the words, "Want to go bye-bye?" which brings a run to the door, knowing a ride in the car with the window down, and head out of it, is coming. It doesn't take a whole lot to please a dog.

A dog is a true companion when one is sick, or lonely, or just wanting to share a time on the path walkway with another. Their presence seems to bring the peace of the Lord. Their protective nature guards the home and family in a way no other sense of duty can. With a keen nose and sensitive ears, they are ready at all times.

With an attitude of thanksgiving, I am glad we have a dog. She is yet another demonstration of the Lord's love for us, and His display of His vast and amazing creativity.

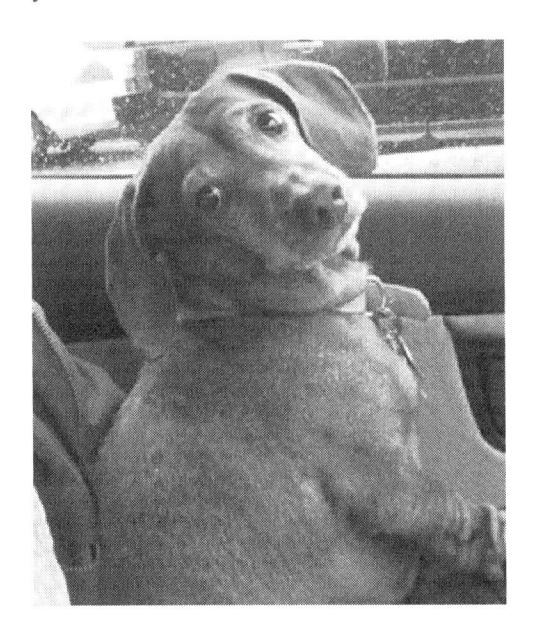

Zoe – our pet Dachshund

19.

Inquire of the Lord Lately?

"David inquired of the Lord, saying, "Shall I pursue this band? Shall I overtake them?" And He said to him, "Pursue, for you will surely overtake them, and you will surely rescue all."(I Samuel 30:8-9 NASU)

In my daily Bible reading I have been appreciating the life of David, and how there is so much for us to be encouraged by how he did it. Even in those times when David was being chased by King Saul, who was out to kill him, David was learning to communicate with the Lord. Getting the basics down would be instrumental in his entire walk, as he himself went on to become the anointed king of Israel.

When I consider my own walk with the Lord, I appreciate the times when I myself inquire of the Lord, to ask Him what His plan is, what He would want me to do, or how I should consider that situation before me. When I do seek Him, He does respond. In His time and place, which all the time is at the exact time needed.

Even a simple ask, like "What now Lord?" will bring a response from Him. It may come in the form of a word from a friend or family member. He may choose to give us a dream. A specific word can come through the prophetic gift being exercised, speaking into our need through another that we may not even know. Or He may direct you to a Bible passage, enlightening a written Scripture in your own daily reading that speaks to your spirit.

Having that relationship with the Lord, of simple communication, shouldn't be an odd thing. Nor should communicating with Him be an occasional thought, or only when we get in desperate situations. If we make it one of our foundational stones, to know His voice, it will be a natural thing to ask, listen, hear and respond accordingly. The Holy Spirit after all was promised to us to be as our Helper, given to abide with us always.

I can recall times when I felt I didn't need to inquire of the Lord. After all, I was old enough to know what to do, right? And yes, at a later point, it could have saved me a lot of trouble if I had. Lesson learned.

"Evil men do not understand justice, but those who seek the Lord understand all." (Proverbs 28:5, NKJV)

In these times of trouble, it is vital that we are comfortable in asking the Lord His thoughts on subjects, and what His heart is. The voices we hear of the many others giving their opinions can drown out the truth, so we need to be able to discern His voice, and abide in His presence.

Have you inquired of the Lord lately? Now may be as good a time as any.

The work of the Lord

20.

Work Is Work

"Let the favor of the Lord our God be upon us; and confirm for us the work of our hands;
Yes, confirm the work of our hands." (Psalm 90:17, NASU)

Let's face it. Work is work. For those of us who are blessed to have a job in this financial climate, and especially one that actually enables one to pay the bills, work is work. It is a must if we are going to feed the family, provide covering, and experience the daily provision that is necessary, day in and day out.

When Adam was kicked out of Eden after the original sin, he no longer had the joy of living in the garden that had been given to him to flourish in. He was then told, as written in Gen 3:17-19, "To Adam he said, "Because you listened to what your wife said and ate from the tree about which I gave you the order, 'You are not to eat from it,' the ground is cursed on your account; you will work hard to eat from it as long as you live. It will produce thorns and thistles for you, and you will eat field plants. You will eat bread by the sweat of your forehead till you return to the ground — for you were taken out of it: you are dust, and you will return to dust." (Complete Jewish Bible)

Work resulted as a result of his disobedience to the Lord. Instead of heeding the instructions to not do something, he went ahead and did it. The consequences still live on for all of mankind.

With over 45 years of work "under my belt", I can say there were times when work was a joy. You can be fulfilled in setting a goal, working hard at completing it, and then receiving the rewards that accompany it. But more often than not, if I am sharing honestly, work was difficult, at times boring, and often not what my heart dreamed of doing. Indeed, the "sweat of your forehead" didn't seem to bring the life many spoke of in the Sunday morning messages. The Monday through Friday job was a necessary, not the choice many of us would have made if given the opportunity.

We seek the Lord to understand the meaning of the job we daily have to put our hands to. We often think of what is the eternal meaning of doing the same tasks that in the long run we wonder why it is done at all. What purpose is accomplished for civilization if what we do today is gone tomorrow? It is a question faced by many as they go about their work.

Solomon felt the frustration, as he wrote this, now recorded in Scripture for all time. "So I hated life, for the work which had been done under the sun was grievous to me; because everything is futility and striving after wind." (Ecclesiastes 2:17, NASU) Something was missing in his life. Futility and strife was all he could see as the result.

For most of us, 50-60 years of work is enough. If that what we have done has brought some good for those around us, we can find fulfillment in what has been accomplished. Trusting in the Lord during that time can be a main hope that His will and purpose for us did occur, and that our reward awaits us in heaven. For those who have not this hope, then what they have done will be gone when they are gone. Burned up forever at that point to come.

I am grateful for the job that I have been given as my trade, and the resulting provision given for this life. But I look forward to that day when all labor has been completed, and the eternal reward awaits.

Understanding the whys and why nots may only be known when we have reached the other side. In the meantime, keeping our eyes on the Lord must be our daily task, while doing our daily tasks.

May it be said of us also, as Jesus prayed, "I glorified You on the earth, having accomplished the work which You have given Me to do." (John 17:4-5, NASU)

21.

The Elections

"Do you want to be on good terms with the government? Be a responsible citizen and you'll get on just fine, the government working to your advantage." (Romans 13:3-4, The Message)

Every four years in American politics the voting age population has a choice to make in the selection of the one who will sit in the presidential office seat. Voting for our elected officials is one of the many freedoms that our founding fathers fought so hard to obtain, and many, many since then have fought to maintain. The freedom to choose is not found in all nations. But in this country, since 1776, it has been one of the great freedoms we have as a people.

Sad to say that too many choose not to exercise this democratic freedom. Since I turned the voting age of 18 in the early 70's, I have not missed a presidential election, going to the voting booth every time. I am proud, if I can say that humbly, to have done that.

The opportunity taken to vote or not to vote was never a decision I considered *not* doing. As a citizen of this nation, while I still abide here, I will always feel it is included as one of my basic responsibilities. No doubt I will continue to vote at every opportunity I have. If I am going to pray for our government leaders (not as much as I should), I believe it is also my responsibility, every time I am given the choice, to also vote for the ones who adhere to the principles I stand for. I find it hard to think that other believers often choose to not participate.

How can those who say they are walking in the Lord's ways not also take the time to know the candidates and then vote for those they want to see lead our local, state, and national offices? Even if our choice we voted for does not win, at least we can say we participated in the process.

Believing that the Lord sets in place those in authority who govern, He also wants us to take part in bringing that about. We are not just to sit it out and say that whatever will be will be, or to glibly say that our actions do not matter in the outcome, so why bother? Does the Lord not tell us to be a light on a hill? Is not the government realm another area where that light is so sorely needed in our time, where we can participate in taking His principles into all areas of life? Even to this one area.

If and when you are given the opportunity, take it, and do one more thing in extending the Lord's kingdom on this earth. As an American, do the right thing, and vote for those who will act on our behalf. As a big election block voting in unison, we carry a lot of influence, and can do a lot of good. Many have gotten elected because of us. Others have lost because we have not done our part.

If we don't exercise this freedom, we cannot rant and rave when the darkness even more so penetrates the halls of our government buildings.

We can participate in what the Lord desires to yet do in this nation. This is one opportunity He freely gives you and me to do, as we go to vote, with His wisdom and guidance leading us.

22.

Let Not Your Heart Grow Cold

"Above everything else, guard your heart; for it is the source of life's consequences." Proverbs 4:23, Complete Jewish Bible)

I had woken up trying to fight off bitterness and resentment in my mind. I didn't want it to overtake my heart.

In the dream I just had, my wife Laurie and I were ushers for a large gathering. I don't recall if it was on a ship, at a conference, or a special church event. It seemed as if we had been part of the "invited guests" list, being a part of the group, but chose to be servants for the others by ushering. We had been doing this for a number of years.

As the dream continued, around 10 pm, when the meeting was over and all had left for the banquet, we too went to get our food, expecting to receive what the others would have gotten earlier. Along the way I passed several tables which had key lime pie available on small plates, as the desert. Thinking I might want a piece before they were gone, I picked up one plate and began eating the slice of pie. (I must have been hungry!)

When I got to the food line, where the food had been set up in cafeteria style for large crowds, all I could see left were turkey wings – basically bones with a little meat on them – and some mashed potatoes. I asked the servers if there was anything else left, and they said no. They were preparing for the next meal, but I couldn't have that.

I then woke up (the red digital lights read 2:22 am on the clock) and I laid there for at least 20 minutes, trying to guard both my mind and my heart from the thoughts of bitterness, anger and resentment that threatened to overtake me. Here we had just served all these people, and yet nothing good was left for us to partake too.

It was a real struggle, as my mind thought back over the years when my service in ministry could at times have been taken for granted. Would I allow this attitude to get the best of me now at this point in my life?

There are three things I felt the Lord was trying to tell me. He may also do the same with you through this dream.

    1. We are in a spiritual battle. In these last days, our hearts can grow cold due to the atmosphere around us, with darkness trying to

constantly overtake everything. We are in a real battle for our souls and those we are in contact with.
2. As we grow older in the faith, and in our bodies, we can become cynical, seeing things happen over and over again, with no change happening. It can wear us down and cause us to pull back from engaging with others, and giving in service to them out of love.
3. If we allow weeds to fall in our spiritual soil and grow roots, they will consume the good wheat that has also been planted. A root of bitterness can destroy your spiritual walk and testimony. "See to it that no one comes short of the grace of God; that no root of bitterness springing up causes trouble, and by it many be defiled;" (Hebrews 12:15, NASU)

Looking back in our faith walk, in order to keep moving forward, if we do not give thanks and continue to see with the Lord's vision, we will give in to that which will steal our joy, our purpose, and our direction in this life. We must keep fighting the good fight, guard our hearts, and pray that they do not grow cold.

Remember, we serve a good God, and He is the Rewarder of those who seek Him. May He find faith when He returns. "But without faith it is impossible to please Him, for he who comes to God must believe that He is, and that He is a rewarder of those who diligently seek Him." (Hebrews 11:6, NKJV)

23.

What To Do

"Be anxious for nothing, but in everything by prayer and supplication with thanksgiving let your requests be made known to God. And the peace of God, which surpasses all comprehension, will guard your hearts and your minds in Christ Jesus." (Philippians 4:6-7 NASU)

If you have access to a TV, radio, newspaper or an Internet connection, then I would imagine that you hear news on a regular basis. And if you are one like I am, you listen to it or search it out to keep up with "what is going on in the world."

The type of reporting you listen to will eventually determine how you react and respond to what is presented in days ahead. For most, they get their news from the major news outlets on cable TV. But with changing viewing habits, more and more are finding good news sources are available and more read and watched on the Internet. You then have a choice as to what "slant" you will get, for nowadays there is little "straight" news published. Most reporting articles lean one way or the other.

With the desire to publish newsworthy truth, as close to what the Bible declares that is, I use many articles from the Internet for our ministry blog *Love For His People*. These are gathered from several sources that I have learned to trust and rely on, that present honest, current and reliable news that most aligns with our beliefs. They include the websites of Charisma News, CBN News, Israel Today, Breaking Israel News, TruNews and The Jim Bakker Show. We also get emails from Michael Snyder (The Economic Collapse Blog), Ron Cantor (Messiah's Mandate in Tel Aviv), and Israel365 (Rabbi Tuly Weisz in Israel) that are reposted on our ministry blog.

Once published on the blog, these articles are then also uploaded to our Facebook, Twitter and other social media outlets we use to get this message out. In this way we hope to keep others updated with articles that other broadcasts or websites don't (or won't) share. As believers in the Lord Jesus Christ, that is very important to us.

Given the enormous verbiage that we each face each day, we must be careful as to what we allow to come into our homes and spiritual lives. It is vital to protect ourselves and those we hold dear and have responsibility for, even as watchmen would do so guarding the entries to homes and cities. Knowing what to do, when situations arise requiring good decisions made, will come out of that which has gone into our spirits. Shifting out the tares to allow wheat seed to grow will bear a good harvest at the right time.

Guarding our hearts and minds, our eternal souls, is becoming even more vital in these days of increasingly biased media, which lacks in reporting news the Holy Spirit would approve of. After all, being He knows all, we need His filtering system to watch over us. That way we will know what to do when we need to have the wisdom and knowledge needed to act accordingly. We will also have the peace of Christ to appropriately walk it out.

Protect yourself from the evils of this world. One way is to get your news from good sources.

24.

History & Truth

"However, when He, the Spirit of truth, has come, He will guide you into all truth; for He will not speak on His own authority, but whatever He hears He will speak; and He will tell you things to come." (John 16:13, NKJV)

Some memories you will never forget, being reminded of them through photos, music, and conversations that are shared at gatherings, or broadcast through other media. They are passed down from generation to generation, retelling the stories that had impact on the lives involved.

History is made that way. Events happen; people want to remember them; they are written down or captured in motion. It is one way to be assured that one never forgets. It is a way to accurately describe what took place then, so another down the road cannot say otherwise.

History books are written to also pass truth from one generation to another. Through these writings, what took place decades or centuries ago are kept recorded lest anyone forget what happened, how it happened, and why it happened. By knowing our history, it hopefully will never be altered by any current pressure to change the facts.

Those who try to rewrite history attempt to break down walls that stand against their lies. If a generation does not know their true history, eventually the lies will prevail, and overcome the historical truth. The walls that stood for truth will fall.

As believers in the Lord Jesus, we are called upon to know the truth. First, truth as recorded in the Scriptures, and also truth of the Lord's work in our nations. If we fail to stand against the attempt of our enemies to destroy truth, what results will be a nation or people so mixed up in their convictions that anything can, and will, develop. Nothing will be held as truth if we neglect to stand for the truth now.

Know your Bible. Know truth. Be strong in your convictions as you stand for what is right. Don't let the enemy keep you from walking in that which you know is righteous and true.

ABOUT THE AUTHOR

Steve Martin served with three Christian ministries from 1987-2010, all having a national and international outreach focus. During that time he made 14 ministry trips to Israel, China, India, Trinidad and Tobago, and the United Kingdom.

On his overseas journeys Steve enjoyed sharing written journal entries with family and friends back home, through Internet media. His light-hearted stories gave an up close and personal touch for those reading along. Many could imagine being there themselves.

His extensive collection of photos taken during these trips, of both local scenery and common people on the streets, has touched thousands through their varied images.

In 2010, Steve and Laurie began *Love For His People, Inc*, a 501©3 non-profit humanitarian aid ministry. This work touches the natural and spiritual lives of those around them with needed encouragement and strength.

Now Think On This!

His regular messages *Now Think On This* are posted on the ministries *Love For His People* and *Now Think of This* blogs. They are also on Facebook and Twitter, featuring words of spiritual enrichment, along with selected photos.

Since 1994, Steve and his good wife Laurie have lived in the Charlotte, NC area, after having homes in Illinois, Michigan and Florida. Now married for more than 39 years, they enjoy their four adult children and spouses (Josh and Chelsie, Ben, Hannah and Jonathan, Christen and Andrew), along with our seven additional grandchildren – Daniel, Logan, Dylan Joy, Jensen, Payton, Jack and Levi Zachary.

While continuing to serve organizations with his accounting skills, he enjoys writing, photography and growing the ministry of *Love For His People, Inc.*

Steve Martin

CONTACT INFORMATION

**Steve Martin
Love For His People, Inc.
12120 WOODSIDE Falls Road
Pineville, NC 28134 USA**

E-mail: loveforhispeople@gmail.com
martinlighthouse@gmail.com

Facebook pages: *Steve Martin* and *Love For His People*

Twitter: *martinlighthous, LovingHisPeople, LoveHisPeople* and *ahavaloveletters*

Blogger: http://loveforhispeople.blogspot.com

YouTube: Steve Martin (loveforhispeopleinc)

Website: www.loveforhispeople.org

Our organization, **Love For His People, Inc.**, is a USA non-profit 501(c)3 ministry.
Fed. ID #27-1633858.

We welcome your gifts and communications of support, as we continue to provide humanitarian aid to our Israel and other connections. We hope you will become connected too along with us, and send a one-time gift or become a regular, monthly friend.

Thank you very much for this consideration!

You can also send checks, or contribute through our PayPal account on our website: http://www.loveforhispeople.org/support.html

We send tax deductible receipts for all gifts received for the work of the ministry!

I hope you enjoyed this book. You can also get my first 12 books, all available on Amazon and from our ministry office. You will see them on the following pages.

Please see our contact information on the prior pages.

When it came time to title this book, I knew it was no coincidence that this was my 12th published work. I count it very special.

Not only is this book my 12th, but there have been other "12s" in my life.

Our home's street address is "12120". My favorite NASCAR driver was "24" – of course, made up of the numbers 2 x 12.

I turned "12 x 5" just over a year and a half ago. Reaching the BIG 60 means I am still going in the Lord's grace and provision!

My 12th trip to Israel occurred in May of 2016. That was very special to me, as my wife joined me for her third trip there. We spent the time with friends whom we help support in the Land.

Being the primary work of our ministry, to bless our Jewish friends in their Promised Land, it was good spending this time in friendship and financial support. Love expressed in both word and deed.

Knowing there are 12 tribes of Israel, 12 apostles selected by Yeshua (Jesus), 12 elders now seated around the throne, 12 months in each year…well, you get the point.

And thus my 12th book, which is another one consisting of 26 *Now Think On This* messages, I counted it yet as another reason for the title *12*.

Martin Lighthouse Publishing, 2016

I share some aspects of how I believe the Bible speaks of love. For you who are about to read this, my prayer is that your heart will be enlarged with His, and you too will become one, even more, to give love for His people, both Jew and Gentile, both saved and unsaved.

I hope that as you read these chapters, you will become more inspired to spend time with the Lord, experience His heart of love, and share it with our fellow man. The world needs to know the love of God.

Martin Lighthouse Publishing, 2015

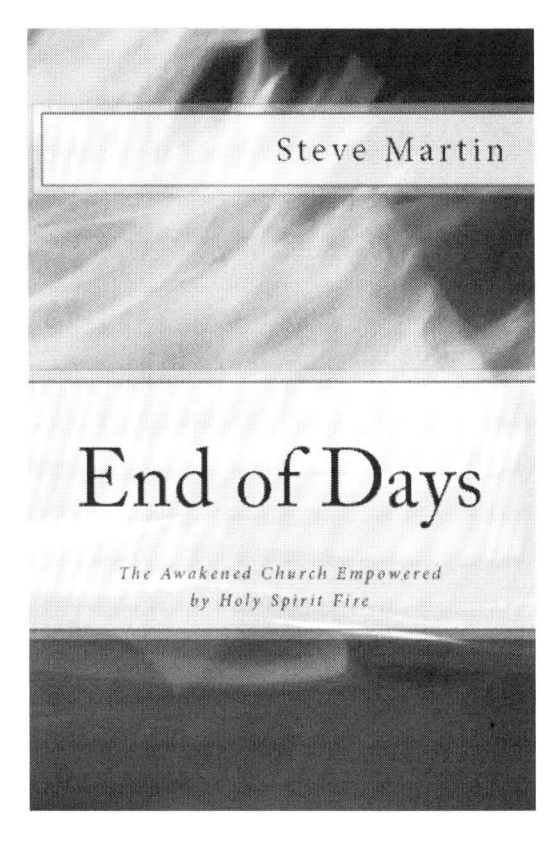

I believe we are living in the end times, the last days, the "End of Days." Beginning in the year of 1948, with the rebirth of Israel, the time clock started ticking. We are seeing prophecy fulfilled as it happens now.

Steve's 10th book Martin Lighthouse Publishing, 2015

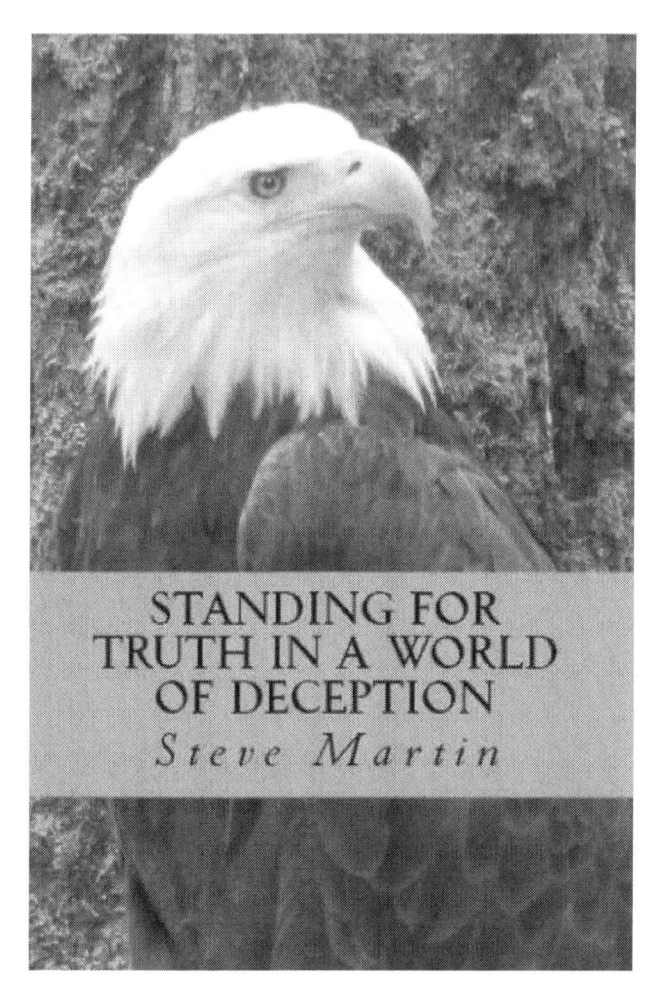

Published in 2015, *Standing For Truth…"* is the 9th book of Steve Martin. It encourages believers to stand for the Word of God in these dark hours.

Martin Lighthouse Publishing, 2015

Published in 2014, *Mountain Top View* is the 8th book of Steve Martin, sharing another copulation of his "Now Think On This" messages.

Martin Lighthouse Publishing, 2014

This is Steve's second in the series of messages – to give hope, encouragement, and share the love of the Lord in your daily walk. Includes more than 165 photos he took in trips to Israel.

Steve Martin's other books all are available on Amazon or from the office of Love For His People.

Martin Lighthouse Publishing, 2014

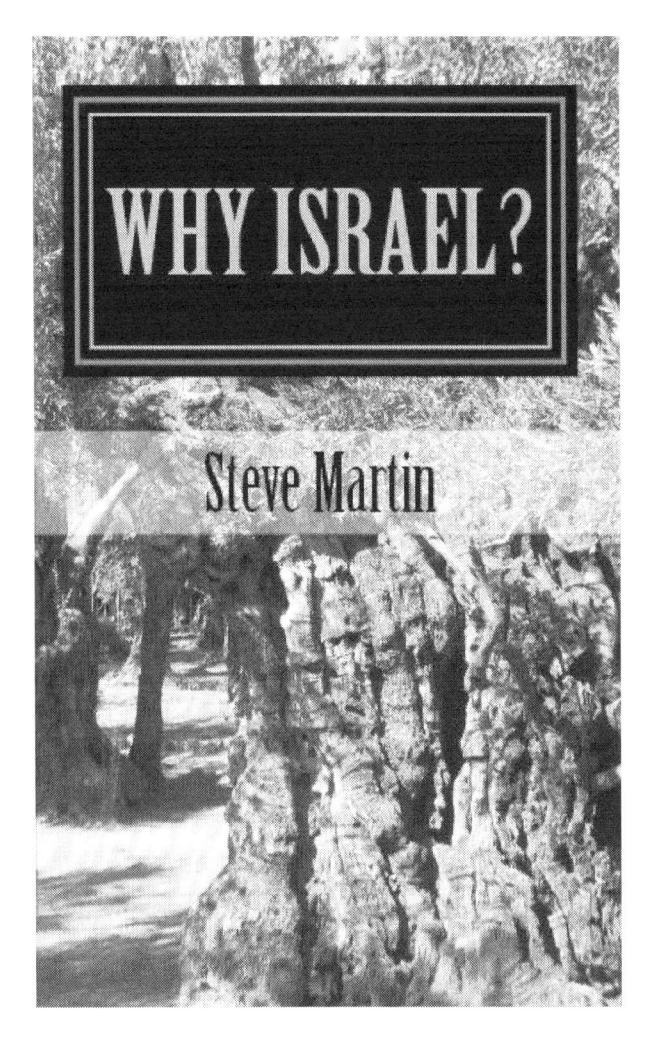

Why Israel? – booklet supporting the fact that the nation of Israel was given to the Jews in fulfillment of the promise made to them centuries by the Lord Himself.

Martin Lighthouse Publishing, 2014

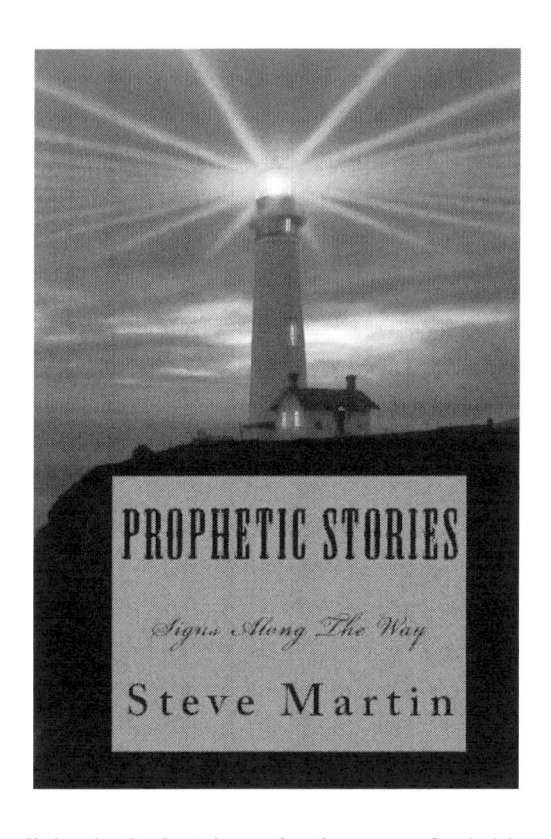

We are living in the last days, the times prophesied long ago, before the Lord Jesus Christ returns. Even as He spoke to the prophets of old in Israel, continuing through Jesus' time on earth, and with the early church, the Lord is fulfilling His promise in His Eternal Word - that He would pour out His Spirit on all flesh, and we would prophesy.

Martin Lighthouse Publishing, 2014

Steve Martin's autobiography about his youth, years with two international ministries, and the journey in-between. Your faith will be encouraged with this one.

Martin Lighthouse Publishing, 2013

After my 10th trip to Israel in 2010, I asked the Lord, "What next?" He said, "Write love letter." And so I did. These are the first 52 of the 150 I have written since then. Read one a day, or one a week.

Xulon Press, 2013

STEVE MARTIN

Author of *The Promise*

Leadership through Love

" Leading and appreciating those who serve with you."

When a person with a prophetic gifting said I should write a book on administration, leadership and management, it only took me 10 years before I did! But it had taken 24 years for me to do it before I could…

Martin Lighthouse Publishing, 2013

**Here are 43 of my NOW THINK ON THIS messages –
to strengthen the hope within, as you press on with His
love through you.**

Martin Lighthouse Publishing, 2013

Stop the Boycott of Israeli Goodies - Buy Israeli Hoodies!

I DID! I DO!

The nations have been practicing anti-Semitism since day one, and now they have started another form of it. Governments in Europe, and now the USA, are enforcing laws stating that any goods produced in the so-called "West Bank" (Judea and Samaria) must carry a label saying "Made in the West Bank", rather than "Made in Israel". Thus any product not having that "West Bank" label will not be sold in their countries.

BDS, "Boycott, Divestment and Sanctions", is at the forefront of this law. It also includes pulling all investments from Israel, in stock, bank deposits, and other financial forms. Sanctions prohibiting purchase of Israeli-produced goods continues to be pushed and accepted in these anti-Semitic nations. All of this is under the guise of supporting a "Palestinian State", or "Palestine".

One way we can combat this, as supporters of Israel, is to buy Israeli goods, direct from the Israeli merchants. Many have a website

for that purpose. You can check the following websites.

We have shown our support for our Israeli friends by purchasing online, and in person when in the land itself, where these goods are produced and sold by our friends. We urge you to do the same.

Here is where I got some of my hoodies, direct from Israel: World of Judaica.com

**Steve Martin, Founder of Love for His People
Israeli IDF Hoodie**

I bought one for each of my son-in-laws (2). They now have an IDF hoodie. My two sons also have them, along with my good wife (Hebrew University logo), daughter (Coca-Cola in Hebrew), grandsons and my one and only granddaughter (IDF hoodies) for kids.

Buy other Israeli-made goods!!!

Shop for items like below
from ISRAEL TODAY.com

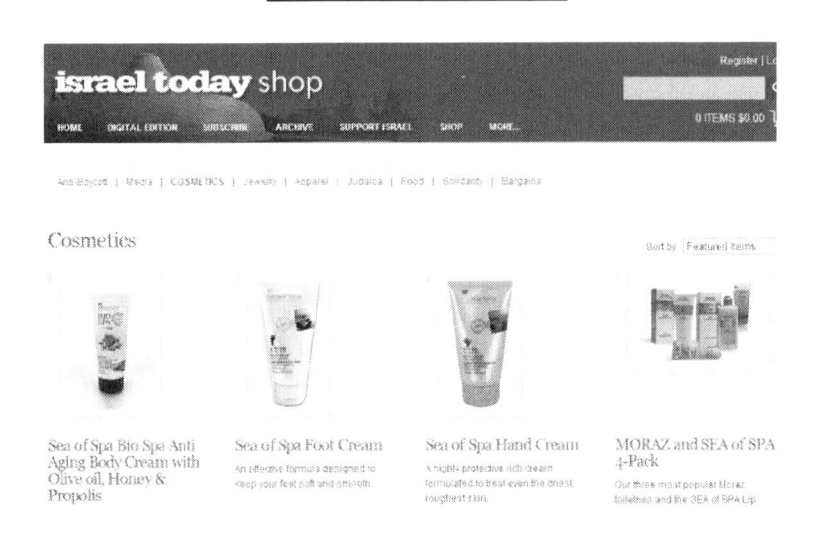

Cosmetics

Sea of Spa Bio Spa Anti Aging Body Cream with Olive oil, Honey & Propolis

Sea of Spa Foot Cream
An effective formula designed to keep your feet soft and smooth

Sea of Spa Hand Cream
A highly protective rich cream formulated to treat even the driest, roughest skin.

MORAZ and SEA of SPA 4-Pack
Our three most popular Moraz toiletries and the SEA of SPA Lip

**Israeli-made hoodie displayed in my home office
Love For His People, Inc.**

**Israeli-made hoodie displayed in my home office
Love For His People, Inc.**

...Where there is no Guidance the people fall.
...But in abundance of counselors there is victory.
באין תחבולות יפול עם
ותשועה ברוב יועץ
MOSSAD
The Institute for Intelligence and Special Operations

**Another Israeli-made hoodie,
with our Dachshund Zoe looking on!**

**Here is where I got my hoodies,
direct from Israel: World of Judaica.com**

And if hoodies are not your thing, here is an Israeli organization we support, having other ISRAELI-MADE goods:

Click here: Israel365 Store with Rabbi Tuly Weisz

We support Israel. We show it by buying Israel-made goods. You can too!

Stop the BDS (Boycott Divestment and Sanctions) boycott of Israel. Buy their goods!

Steve Martin
Founder
Love For His People, Inc.
Charlotte, NC USA

P.S. We receive "no commission" or other remuneration for this. We just support Israel and want to see our Jewish friends blessed. I hope you do too, and act on it.

Or buy Israeli-made watches.
(This is one I wear all the time.)

You can buy at IsraeliProducts.com

ישוע המשיח

Yeshua the Messiah

Special rings made in Israel.

Star of David ring on my hand since 2007. Bought on Ben Yehuda Street at Dan & David Jerusalem, Israel

My hand in Gideon's Pool, Israel 2008

Made in the USA
Middletown, DE
04 June 2017